Elegy for Mary Turner

V
VERSO
London • New York

Elegy for Mary Turner: An Illustrated Account of a Lynching

by

Rachel Marie-Crane Williams

Introduction by Mariame Kaba

Afterword by Julie Buckner Armstrong

Postscript by C. Tyrone Forehand

All royalties from this book will go to the National Center for
Civil and Human Rights in Atlanta, Georgia

First published by Verso 2021
© Rachel Marie-Crane Williams 2021
Introduction © Mariame Kaba 2021
Afterword © Julie Buckner Armstrong 2021
Postscript © C. Tyrone Forehand

1 3 5 7 9 10 8 6 4 2

Verso
UK: 6 Meard Street, London W1F 0EG
US: 20 Jay Street, Suite 1010, Brooklyn, NY 11201
versobooks.com

Verso is the imprint of New Left Books

ISBN-13: 978-1-78873-904-7
ISBN-13: 978-1-78873-907-8 (US EBK)
ISBN-13: 978-1-78873-906-1 (UK EBK)

British Library Cataloguing in Publication Data
A catalogue record for this book is available from the British Library

Library of Congress Cataloging-in-Publication Data
A catalog record for this book is available from the Library of Congress

Typeset in Fournier by Biblichor Ltd, Edinburgh
Printed and bound by CPI Group (UK) Ltd, Croydon CR0 4YY

Contents

Acknowledgments

A special thanks to Rylie and Jack Kelley, who allowed me to skip suppers and take over our dining room for almost two years making prints. A huge and mushy thank you to Don Ward, my partner. I also want to thank Charles and Sharon Williams for helping me finish this project by allowing me to work at Dauntless Wood. To Mariame Kaba, an ongoing light and muse, Julie Buckner Armstrong for cheering me on and encouraging me to look and look again. I want to thank Julie Bowland, Deborah Davis, Teresa Mangum, Steve McGuire, Leslie Schwalm, Laura Kastens, Valdosta State University, the Englert Theater, and the Obermann Center for Advanced Studies and the University of Iowa for their generosity and care. I want to thank Audrey Grant, Mark Patrick George, the Mary Turner Project, and Mr. Charles Tyrone Forehand for telling me wonderful stories and being a ray of sunshine at the end of a long journey, Jessie Kindig, who took a chance and who has been so helpful in making this book better and better, finally, Mark Martin (not the race car driver) and the staff of Verso Books. I also want to thank the Library of Congress, the National Museum of Women in the Arts, and the amazing librarians and archivists who helped me along the way.

Text Sources

My account of events is based primarily on Walter White's article, "The Work of a Mob," in *Crisis* Vol. 16 (September 1918).

Newspaper clippings are from the archives held at the Library of Congress: *Atlanta Constitution*, May 18, 1918 and May 24, 1918; *Atlanta Journal*, May 24, 1918.

The telegrams, letter from Governor Hugh Dorsey, and clipping from the *New York Tribune* are from images taken in the Library of Congress Archives, NAACP collection, Box II L7, Box I C336, Box I C337, Group Series I, Series C, Box 353, Part I C:428, and Part I C:432.

The farmer's almanac is from the 1918 *Illustrated Barker's Almanac* printed by the Barker, Moore &

Mein Medicine Co. in Philadelphia, Pennsylvania.

The postcards are from Valdosta, Georgia, and were printed by an unknown company before 1918. The photos, baby shoes, and letters are from sellers on Ebay. The wood-grain paper is Nepalese Lokta gold and cream woodgrain from Dick Blick.

Rachel Marie-Crane Williams, 2020

Introduction: Say Her Name
— 1918, 1949, 2021 —
Mary Turner and the "Wife of the Victim"

by Mariame Kaba

Untangle the spitting men from the mob
Unsay the word *nigger*
Release the firer's finger from its trigger
Return the revolver to its quiet holster
Return the man to his home
Unwidow his wife

"Reverse: A Lynching," Ansel Elkins

In doing some research about the history of lynching in the United States a few years ago, I came across a haunting photograph.

I found it in a book about an exhibit by Marion Palfi. Palfi called herself a "social research photographer" and documented poverty and oppression in America through her work. The photograph was titled "Irwington, 1949, Wife of the Victim." I was curious about the provenance of the photograph so I did some digging. The caption that accompanied it quotes the wife as saying: "Caleb was a good man . . . he believed in his rights and therefore died." But who was Caleb?

Caleb Hill Jr. was a twenty-eight-year-old Black chalk-miner living in a rural town called Irwinton, Georgia. He was a family man who cared for a wife, three children, mother, father, and two sisters. By all accounts, Caleb Hill was a hard worker and had a stubborn streak. He refused to back down from confrontation.

On the morning of March 30, 1949, Hill, who had been jailed the night before after an altercation, was kidnapped from his cell and later found dead. He had been shot several times and been badly beaten. Caleb Hill was lynched.

The *New York Times* published several articles about this case because the FBI became involved. The initial story told by Sheriff George Hatcher was that Caleb Hill grabbed his gun and shot at him as he was being arrested. Hatcher added that Hill had a terrible reputation and had been arrested several times before. The jail was located on the second floor of the Sheriff's home. He explained that while he was asleep two white men kidnapped Hill. He claimed to have no leads as to who the kidnappers were.

The *New York Times* captured the reaction of the citizens of Irwinton, a town of less than 1,000 people, by quoting one person saying, "It's just a Negro," and another commenting that the incident "didn't upset a checkers game."

Two men were eventually arrested a few days after the lynching. They were Dennis Lamar Purvis (thirty-seven) and Malcolm Vivian Pierce (twenty-seven). One of the men turned out to be the cousin of the sheriff. However, this pair spent only nine days in jail before being freed by an all-white grand jury, which ruled that there wasn't enough evidence for a trial.

Between 1892 and 1940, over 3,000 people, overwhelmingly Black (2,600), were lynched in the United States. In the 1890s, lynchings "claimed an average of 139 lives each year, 75 percent of them Black," according to historian Leon Litwack in *Without Sanctuary*. The decades spanning the early 1880s through the early 1930s have been called the "lynching era" by some historians. This is a period of American history that many people think they understand and yet have never actually studied.

According to her biographer Paula Giddings, journalist and activist Ida B. Wells theorized that "lynching was a direct result of the gains Blacks were making throughout the South." In her autobiography *Crusade for Justice*, Wells wrote, "lynching was merely an excuse to get rid of the Negroes who were acquiring wealth and property and thus keep the race terrorized and 'keep the nigger down'." Backed by a criminal punishment system that maintained and enforced white power and supremacy, Black people were subjugated, oppressed, and exploited. Black people who were lynched were usually first tortured and then once they were dead, their bodies were often mutilated. Sometimes the lynchers would drop the dead Black person's remains on the doorsteps of other Blacks in the community as a warning that if they got out of line they too could meet this fate. It was racist intimidation and terror, pure and simple.

When we bother to remember the victims of lynching in the United States at all, we usually think of Black men. While it is true that the majority of those lynched in America were in fact Black and male, Black women were also disproportionately targeted. In fact, writes Dr. Trichita M. Chestnut for the US National Archives, "Between 1837 and 1946, 173 women were victims of white mob violence in the United States. Of the 173 women lynched: 144 were African American, 25 were white, 3 were Mexican, and 1 was Native American."

One of the women lynched by a Southern white mob is the subject of this book: nineteen-year-old Mary Turner. Turner's name is etched in history in part because of the unspeakable brutality and cruelty of her murder in May 1918. She was eight months pregnant at the time. Her lynching is also known to us today because it was the subject of an NAACP investigation led by Walter White.

Rachel Marie-Crane Williams's project reinserts Mary Turner into our modern retelling of the history of lynching. Turner's story disrupts prior narratives about lynching as we see that it wasn't a punishment for Black beastly men raping white virginal women. An argument over labor and the lynching of her husband Hayes precipitated Turner's brutal murder. Several hundred people watched as Mary was hung upside down, her fetus cut from her womb and crushed beneath the boots of some of the participants. She was shot, mutilated, and set on fire. Her death was truly horrific. The lynchers were never held accountable for their barbaric crime.

In this particular historical moment, when young Black people in particular are engaged in a renewed struggle against state violence including police killings and mass incarceration, Mary Turner's story resonates. As organizers today insist that we must #SayHerName in reference to the Black women (cis and trans) whose lives are cut short by state-sanctioned violence, Mary Turner calls out to us from the grave. She insists that we #SayHerName too. She reminds us that Black women have always been subjects of unlimited and unaccountable violence at the hands of white people.

Caleb Hill Jr.'s wife was left behind to deal with the trauma of his lynching. She was made a widow, and we don't know her name. She is memorialized in a photograph as "wife of the victim." Though nameless, invisible, and silenced, she is also a Black woman victimized by lynching. It would be good to be able to #SayHerName too in order to honor her loss. Rachel's book demands that we expand the scope of who the victims of lynching were beyond those killed. Families and entire communities were impacted, too. In this way, the book fits into a feminist tradition of storytelling.

The lynching of Mary Turner illustrates how Black people (including Black women) have been targeted by extremely cruel violence and punishment throughout our history. Her murder by a white mob was a product of US slave history and also set a pattern for current racial violence. While lynching is a historically specific form of racial terrorism, racist violence still exists against Blacks in 2021. The historical debasement of Black bodies continues. We have always been considered killable and disposable. This remains true today. We still have a culture in this country that sanctions the violation of Black bodies often with impunity.

Elegy for Mary Turner, with its exquisite and emotional art, is incredibly relevant today. It is a lament for the dead and a call for memorialization of the living. It is art that elicits blinding rage and offers an opportunity to grieve. I have told Mary's story to Black girls as young as thirteen years old as a way to explain the legacy of US slavery, Reconstruction, and racialized gender violence. Rachel's work will be a mainstay in my teaching and organizing going forward. In her haunting poem "Reverse: A Lynching" that opened this essay, Ansel Elkins imagines undoing a lynching so that we might "reenter the night through its door of mercy." Rachel's book about Mary Turner offers no mercy but it does push us toward accountability. This is what's needed now more than ever.

This book is dedicated to all the victims of lynching in the United States, but especially to the women and children. Below is an incomplete list of recorded female victims lynched between 1886 and 1957. All of the women on this list were Black; some of the women were pregnant, mothers, and wives. All of them were murdered.

Mrs. John Sims
Mrs. Hawkins
Mr. Hawkins
Mrs. Ben French
Maria Smith
Milly Thompson
Julia Brandt
Anna Eliza Cowan
Harriet Finch
Mary Hollenbeck
Eliza Wood
Ms. Cummins
Gracy Blanton
Roxie Elliot
Mrs. Lee
Eliza Lowe
Ella Williams
Louisa Stevenson
Mrs. Martin
Mrs. Brisco
Jessie Dillingham
Ella
Mrs. Hastings
Mrs. Hastings
Cora
Jessie Jones
Meredith Lewis
Emma Fair
Louisa Carter
Mahala Jackson
Mrs. Phil Evans
Mary Elizabeth Motlow
Rilla Weaver
X
Marion Howard

Harriet Talley
Mary Deane
Alice Green
Martha Green
Mollie Smith
Mrs. Abe Phillips
Hannah Phillips
X
Mrs. James Mason
X
Felicia Francis
Hannah Kearse
Charlotte Morris
Isadora Morley
Mimm Collier
X
Otla Smith
Amanda Franks
Molly White
Dora Baker
Rose Etheridge
Eliza Goode
Willia Boyd
Mrs. Jim Cross
Mr. Cross
Lizzie Pool
Anna Mabley
X
Ballie Crutchfield
Terry Bell
Betsy McCray
Ida McCray
X
Bell Duly
Mrs. Emma Wideman
X
X

Lamb Whittle
Jennie Steers
Jennie McCall
Mrs. Holbert
Marie Thompson
X
Meta Hicks
X
X
Mrs. Padgett
Mrs. Padgett
Mrs. D. Walker
Mr. Walker
Robley Baskin
Emile Antoine
Laura Mitchell
Laura Porter
Laura Nelson
Hattie Bowman
Mr. Pettigrew
Mrs. Pettigrew
X
Belle Hathaway
X
Mary Jackson
Ann Boston
Mrs. Joe Perry
Marie Scott
Jennie Collins
Paralee Collins
Rosa Richardson
Jane Sullivan
Ella Charles
Ella Charles
B. Riley

Cordelia Stevenson
Mary Dennis
Stella Long
Mary Conley
Emma Hooper
Sarah Caliness
Mrs. James Eyer
Alma House
X
X
Minnie Looney
Rachel Moore
Mercy Hall
Sarah Carrier
Listy Gordon
X
X
Penny Westmoreland
Sheldon
Sarah Williams
Annie Lowman
Lily Cabb
Eliza Bryant
Bertha Lowman
Sally Brown
X
X
Laura Wood
Viola Dial
Mrs. Zane Eyere
Hally White
Mrs. Wise
Dorothy Malcolm
Mae Dorsey
Angenora Spencer
Mrs. Frank Clay

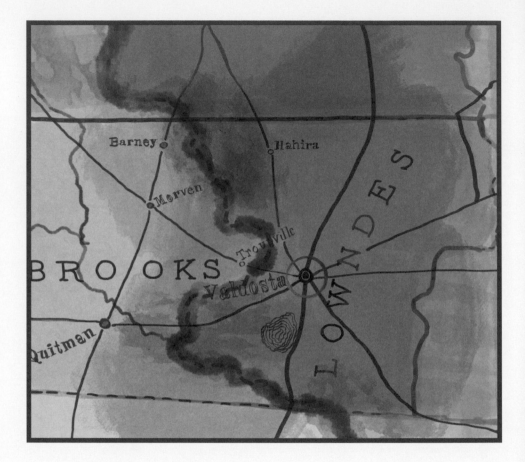

In 1918 between the 17th and 24th of May in the Southern part of Georgia, specifically in Brooks and Lowndes County, a mob lynched 10 men and one woman. The woman was pregnant. Her name was

Mary Turner

STREET.   VALDOSTA, GA.

5th Month — MAY 1918 — 31 Days

Days Month	Days Week	Sun Rises h. m.	Sun Sets h. m.	Sun Fast m.	Moon Rises h. m.	Moon Constel'n c.	Moon Constel'n d.	Moon Souths h. m.	Aspects of Planets, Etc.	High Tide Philadelphia Morn	High Tide Philadelphia Even
1	Wed.	5 1	6 53	3	11 55		13	4 2	St. Philip and St. James	5 8	5 32
2	Thu.	5 0	6 54	3	morn		26	4 56	Regulus S. 7h 24m A	5 56	6 21
3	Fri.	4 59	6 55	3	0 33		10	5 48	3 Venus rises 3h 12m M	6 47	7 14
4	Sat.	4 57	6 56	3	1 7		24	6 39	☌ ♅ ☾	7 42	8 13
Rogation Sunday									**Day's Length: 14h. 1m.**		
5	Sun.	4 56	6 57	3	1 39		8	7 30	Denebola S. 8h 52m A	8 45	9 17
6	Mon.	4 55	6 58	3	2 10		23	8 21	Mars sets 2h 41m M	9 48	10 19
7	Tue.	4 54	6 59	4	2 42		7	9 13	☌ ♀ ☾	10 50	11 20
8	Wed.	4 53	7 0	4	3 15		22	10 7	☾ in perigee	11 49	....
9	Thu.	4 51	7 1	4	3 52		7	11 4	Ascension Day : ☌ ☿ ☾	0 17	0 45
10	Fri.	4 50	7 2	4	sets		22	ev. 3	10 ☿ in aphelion	1 10	1 34
11	Sat.	4 49	7 3	4	8 45		6	1 3	Spica S. 10h 5m A	2 1	2 28
Sunday after Ascension									**Day's Length: 14h. 16m.**		
12	Sun.	4 48	7 4	4	9 44		20	2 3	☌ ♃ ☾ : ☾ in ☋	2 55	3 21
13	Mon.	4 47	7 5	4	10 34		4	3 0	☾ gr. libration W.	3 46	4 11
14	Tue.	4 47	7 6	4	11 15		17	3 54	Arcturus S. 10h 44m A	4 36	5 1
15	Wed.	4 46	7 7	4	11 50		0	4 44	☌ ♆ ☾	5 24	5 46
16	Thu.	4 45	7 8	4	morn		13	5 30	☌ ♄ ☾	6 8	6 29
17	Fri.	4 44	7 9	4	0 21		25	6 13	17 Jupiter sets 8h 49m A	6 51	7 13
18	Sat.	4 43	7 10	4	0 47		7	6 55	Alphacca S. 11h 47m A	7 37	8 1
Pentecost—Whit Sunday									**Day's Length: 14h. 28m.**		
19	Sun.	4 42	7 10	4	1 11		19	7 36	□ ♅ ☉ : ☌ ♂ ☾	8 27	8 53
20	Mon.	4 41	7 11	4	1 36		1	8 17	☾ in apogee	9 18	9 43
21	Tue.	4 40	7 12	4	2 1		12	8 59	Saturn sets 0h 4m M	10 8	10 33
22	Wed.	4 39	7 13	4	2 27		24	9 42	Antares S. 0h 28m M	10 58	11 22
23	Thu.	4 39	7 14	3	2 56		7	10 29	Uranus rises 0h 43m M	11 47	....
24	Fri.	4 38	7 15	3	3 29		19	11 18	☿ gr. elong. W., 25° 12′	0 12	0 35
25	Sat.	4 38	7 16	3	rises		1	morn	25 Neptune sets 11h 26m A	0 57	1 18
Trinity Sunday									**Day's Length: 14h. 40m.**		
26	Sun.	4 37	7 17	3	8 18		14	0 10	♀ in perihelion	1 40	2 4
27	Mon.	4 36	7 18	3	9 9		27	1 3	☾ in ☊	2 28	2 52
28	Tue.	4 36	7 18	3	9 54		10	1 58	☾ gr. libration E.	3 16	3 40
29	Wed.	4 35	7 19	3	10 35		23	2 52	Vega S. 2h 10m M	4 4	4 28
30	Thu.	4 35	7 19	3	11 10		7	3 45	Corpus Christi	4 52	5 15
31	Fri.	4 34	7 20	3	11 42		21	4 36	☿ gr. hel. lat. S.	5 38	6 2

MOON'S PHASES—Eastern Standard Time

☾ Last Quarter, ... 3d. 5h. 26m. A. | ☽ First Quarter, ...17d. 3h. 14m. A.
● New Moon, ...10d. 8h. 1m. M. | ○ Full Moon, ...25d. 5h. 32m. A.

Weather Forecasts—1-3, generally stormy; 4-5, clear and cool; 6-8, clear, high wind, frosty; 9-11, little rain, clearing cool; 12-14, mild and pleasant; 15-16, cloudy, rain; 17-18, quite warm, high wind; 19-20, cool and frosty; 21-22, warm and pleasant; 23-24, little rain; 25-26, clear, high wind; 27-28, pleasant; 29-30, clear and warm.

It began in Brooks County.
Hampton Smith, a plantation
owner, often found farm labor
in the form of black men who
were arrested and convicted.
These men were sentenced to jail,
or ordered to pay a fine.

Smith would pay their fines
in return for indentured
servitude on his cotton plantation.

Sidney Johnson, who had been fined $30.00 for gaming had worked on Smith's plantation in order to pay his debt. Johnson and Smith quarreled over wages and Johnson's obligations. Smith, a ruthless and unfair employer, physically beat Johnson.

Johnson swore revenge.

Hampton Smith

A few nights later, Hampton Smith was killed instantly by a bullet shot through his window. His wife was also struck; the shooter narrowly missed taking her life. The bullet passed very close to her heart.

When Mrs. Smith was shot,
she was pregnant.

Mrs. Smith recovered from the shooting and later
had Hampton Smith's
child!

After the shootings...

White men and boys came
together from Brooks and
Lowndes counties as rumors
of conspiracy, robbery, black men
with guns, and cold-blooded
murder raced through the
community. They formed a mob
and began their hunt with a thirst
for blood and violence.

SOUTH GEORGIA FARMER IS SHOT FROM AMBUSH

Wife Then Dragged From House and Shot Through the Shoulder.

Valdosta, Ga., May 17.—Hampton Smith, a young farmer living near Barney, in Brooks county, was shot and killed by an assassin firing through the window of his home after supper last night, as he stood on the floor. Two shots were fired.

Mrs. Smith ran through the house to the door and was jerked out on the ground and sbo tthrough the shoulder. She ran through the field to a small branch and remained in hiding for two hours, when she went to the home of a negro family and reported the tragedy. Mrs. Smith recognized a young negro named Sidney Johnson, who had been working for her husband two or three weeks, going there from Valdosta.

The shooting was done with Mr. Smith's rifle, which was stolen while he and his wife were at supper. It was about midnight before news of the tragedy reached the white neighbors, who had been scouring the country for the murderer. Dogs from the convict camp of this county were sent there soon after the tragedy was reported.

Mrs. Smith's injuries are not serious. The motive for the murder is not known. Mr. and Mrs. Smith have been married only a short while. She is a very pretty woman.

Murderer Located in Swamp

At 5 o'clock this evening, Sheriff Nix and a posse from Berrien county with track dogs reached Valdosta to assist the officers and posses from Lowndes and Brooks counties in the search for the negroes. Sid Johnson was traced to his former home near Valdosta, but escaped from the posse. His wife was believed to have sheltered him and assisted him in making his escape as officers were gathering to storm the house. She has been arrested and jailed.

At 6:20 this evening a message came from Sheriff Nix that his dogs had run the negro to cover in a swamp several miles southeast of Valdosta. He asked for assistance in capturing him. Fifty men or more have gone to the scene, and it is probable that the murderer will be captured during the night.

THREE NEGROES ARRESTED; LYNCHING ALMOST CERTAIN

Moultrie, Ga., May 17.—(Special.)—Three of the five negroes who killed Hampton Smith, a prominent Brooks county farmer, at his home near Bar-

ney last night and assaulted and shot his wife, have been captured, a telephone message received here states. The men will be carried before Mrs. Smith for identification, but her condition is such that it is hardly probable that she will be able to look them over. Three of the five men were farm hands on the Smith place.

Three of the men were captured late today and it is believed that the other two have been located. One of the negroes under arrest is said to have admitted being connected with the crime.

Feeling around Barney is high and a lynching is considered certain if Mrs. Smith identifies the men who have been caught. Several hundred citizens of Brooks, Conquitt and Lowndes counties made up the posses that conducted the hunt for the negroes. Sidney Johnson is one of those who has not been arrested. He is said to be armed with a Winchester rifle, and at Barney it was considered doubtful that he could be taken alive.

Mrs. Smith has no chance to recover, it is stated.

Will Head   Will Thompson

On Friday, May 17th, outside of Barney, Georgia Will Head was seized by the mob. Later in the afternoon, Will Thompson was also seized by the mob. Both men were lynched that night in Troupeville, Georgia by the mob. The bodies of the dead men were shot by members of the mob, over 700 times.

On May 18th, Hayes Turner, a man who had served time on the chaingang for an altercation with Hampton Smith, was captured and held at the Quitman jail. A sheriff and clerk of court were transporting him to Moultrie, Georgia when the mob stopped the car and took him. They lynched him near the crossroad of Morven and Barney. His hands were still cuffed behind his back.

His body remained tied to the tree branches for two days. Curious white people came from miles around on Sunday to look upon his corpse. On Monday, the body of Hayes Turner was cut down and buried by men serving time in the county jail.

Eugene Rice

On the same day that Hayes
Turner was lynched, Saturday,
May 18th, another man was
lynched near Morven. His
name was reported as Eugene
Rice. He had no connection
to Hampton Smith.

A week after the lynchings began, the bodies of three black men were found in the Little River.

It was unknown if they were
Victims of the mob violence or
casualties from an earlier time.

Their bodies disappeared
again, soon after they
were found.

Little River.
ALDOSTA, Ga.

On Sunday, May 19th 1918
Mary Turner, who was
married to Hayes Turner,
spoke out against his lynching.
She bravely called for justice
through the courts for his
murder.

By noon, Mary Turner
was seized by the mob.
The men who seized her
were determined to, "teach her
a lesson".

Mary Turner was eight months
pregnant.

Mary Turner's feet were
bound and she was hung
from the branch of an oak tree
near the Folsom Bridge,
over the Little River. The
mob doused her in gasoline
and set fire to her body.

Mary Turner

When the fire had burned away her clothing, a man took a large butcher knife and slit open her pregnant belly. The child fell from her open, empty, womb to the ground.

Baby 17 Turner

The baby cried out. A man stepped forward from the mob and crushed the newborn's fragile skull with the heel of his heavy boot.

Finally, the mob of men and boys shot at the corpse of Mary Turner, filling her burnt, bloody, body with hundreds of bullets.

WOMAN LYNCHED BY BROOKS CO. MOB

Mary Turner, Wife of Hayes Turner, Hanged Saturday Night, Met Same Fate Sunday Afternoon, Making Fifth Victim.

Valdosta, Ga., May 19.—Mary Turner, wife of Hayes Turner, was hanged this afternoon at Folsom's bridge over Little river, about sixteen miles north of Valdosta. Hayes Turner was hanged at the Okapilco river in Brooks county last night. His wife, it is claimed made unwise remarks today about the execution of her husband and the people in their indignant mood took exceptions to her remarks, as well as her attitude, and without waiting for nightfall took her to the river where she was hanged and her body riddled with bullets.

It is also claimed that a gold watch belonging to the murdered man, Hampton Smith, was found in her possession and that the plot to kill had been laid in her house.

This makes five persons lynched in this section as a result of the Smith tragedy at Barney. All of Sydney Johnson's relatives, including his mother and father, were landed in jail here last night. Tonight, owing to the increased feeling among the people, the jail is being strongly guarded to prevent trouble. Besides the chase after Sidney Johnson, posses are tonight looking for other negroes in this section and feeling among both white and black seems to be growing more intense.

On Thursday night two negroes stole a shotgun from Hampton Smith at Barney and shot and killed Smith in his home. Mrs. Smith fled from the house and was attacked. She awoke the following morning in a creek and went to a negro cabin for aid. Those who investigated her story found Smith's body and the negroes, farm hands, had disappeared.

Since then the farming section of that part of the state has been greatly aroused.

A double guard was placed around the jail tonight.

It was learned tonight that posses are searching for still another negro besides Johnson, known as Julius. This negro, it was said, aided Johnson to escape from the posse last night.

NEGRO WOMAN IS HANGED BY BROOKS COUNTY MOB

Was Wife of One of the Men Implicated in the Smith Murder

VALDOSTA, Ga., May 20.—Mary Turner, wife of Hayes Turner, was hanged Sunday afternoon at Folsom's bridge over Little river, about sixteen miles north of Valdosta. Hayes Turner was hanged at the Okapilco river in Brooks county Saturday night. His wife, it is claimed, made unwise remarks today about the hanging of her husband and the people took exceptions to her remarks, as well as her attitude, and without waiting for nightfall took her to the river, where she was hanged and her body riddled with bullets.

It is also claimed that a gold watch belonging to Hampton Smith, was found in her possession, and that the plot to kill had been laid in her house.

This makes four persons lynched in this section as a result of the Smith tragedy at Barney. All of Sydney Johnson's relatives, including his mother and father, were landed in jail here Saturday night. Owing to the increased feeling among the people, the jail is being strongly guarded to prevent trouble. Besides the chase after

White residents knew of the violence and death. Many were upset, some were ashamed. But, they had pies to bake; they had hogs to feed. Their lives moved forward.

They minded their own business. On Sunday they prayed. Some spoke quietly to each other; they felt fear and shame. A few felt like it was all part of the natural order. They had the responsibility of dominion. They had to protect their women and the purity of the white race.

The Black men, women and children
tried to avoid the notice and anger
of the white vigilantes. They had
spent generations living in a climate
of intense terror and fear. They
knew they could never let down their
guard.

N.Y. Tribune, May 22, 1918

Georgia's Lynch Law

Even amid all the war horrors of which we must read daily until we grow a little callous it is permissible to express some horror at the lynching of a colored woman in Georgia. Her crime was apparently her vehement denunciation of the lynching of her own husband the day before on the mere accusation of being concerned in the murder of a white man. It will be observed that here was no suggestion of a crime committed, nor the remotest connection with the one crime which is supposed to condone these barbarous performances in the South.

Dr. Moton, president of Tuskegee Institute, has given wide publicity to the fact that from one-quarter to one-third of the lynchings of negroes occur in the State of Georgia. In 1916, the last year for which we have seen figures, fourteen out of fifty-four were in that state.

In 1916 all save one of the fifty-four lynchings were in Southern states and fifty of the victims were negroes. Attorney General Gregory's state, Texas, stood second to Georgia, with a total of nine. Only one in four of the fifty-four was for the crime of rape.

19. Chime Riley

Chime Riley, was lynched
by the mob. They bound
his hands and feet, weighted
down his body with clay
cups used to collect sap
from pine trees to make
turpentine, and threw him
into the Little River. There
was no connection between
Chime Riley and the shooting
Of Hampton Smith.

Simon Schuman

Simon Schuman, another Black man, who was not connected to Hampton Smith, was called to his front door in Berlin, Georgia in Kolquitt County. It was in the evening between eight and nine o'clock. He was forced from his home. His family fled in terror as the mob smashed his furniture and destroyed the inside of the home. His body was never found.

Sidney Johnson

Sidney Johnson, who was responsible
for the murder of Hampton Smith, was
found in Valdosta. The Chief of Police
took a posse of men and surrounded
the house where Johnson was hiding. Both
parties exchanged fire; Johnson was killed.
The crowd rushed the house and dragged
out Johnson's lifeless corpse. They cut off
his penis and threw it in the street. Next,
they tied his body behind a car and dragged
it down Patterson street in Valdosta.
The mangled corpse was then tied to a tree
in Barney and set alight. What remained
was charred to a crisp.

After the lynchings,

Miss C_____

R.F.D. #5 Box 32,
Darlington, S.C.
Aug. 3, 1918.
My dearest Husband,
My thoughts
are now and have been of
you and you alone since I
saw you last.
I arrived in Darl-
ington Thursday A.m. and
have been spending the time
very pleasant despite of the
unfavorable weather.
I only wish for you, I want
to see you of course I do. why
shouldn't I when you are
now and ever shall be dear

African - Americans lived in fear of
violence and death. Over 500 people
left the area.

WESTERN UNION TELEGRAM

NEWCOMB CARLTON, PRESIDENT   GEORGE W. E. ATKINS, FIRST VICE-PRESIDENT

Form 1206

Receiver's No.

Check

Send the following telegram, subject to the terms
on back hereof, which are hereby agreed to

June 3, 1918

John R. Shillady,
C./O Theodore C. Carter,
Wilberforce, O.

LETTER TODAY FROM FRIEND IN ATLANTA WHO WAS IN VALDOSTA AT TIME OF
RECENT LYNCHINGS STATES THAT SMITH WAS KILLED OVER TROUBLE FOLLOWING
CRAP GAME. STATES THAT PRO GERMAN INFLUENCES GIVEN AS JUSTIFICATION.
HE STRONGLY URGES INVESTIGATION. WHAT ACTION DO YOU SUGGEST ISSUING
PRESS STORY TODAY LYNCHING OF SIX IN TEXAS SATURDAY TO ALL PAPERS.

                                        Walter F. White.

Walter F. White was born in Atlanta, Georgia
230 miles from Valdosta. In 1918, just
two years after he graduated from college,
he became an Assistant Secretary
at the N.A.A.C.P., an organization he would
later lead. He was a black man with blonde
hair, blue eyes, and fair skin. This made
it possible for him to infiltrate and
investigate racist groups and racist
communities.

On July 10th, 1918, Walter F. White submitted, in person, a memorandum which stated, in detail, the events and chronology of the lynching spree in Lowndes and Brooks counties. In the memorandum he writes:

> The following names were given to me as being the names of men who were members of the mob, by a man who stated that he himself was a member:
>
> Ordley Yates, Clerk in the post office,
> Frank Purvis, Employed by Griffin Furniture Company,
> Fulton DeVane, Stock Dealer and Auditor and agent for Standard Oil Company,
> _____ Chalmers, Farmer near Quitman,
> Lee Sherrill, Farmer near Quitman,
> Brown Sherrill, Employed by W.A. Whipple,
> Richard DeVane, Farmer,
> Ross DeVane, Farmer, Quitman, G.A.
> _____ Van, Barker, Quitman, G.A.
> Dixon Smith, Brother of Hampton Smith,
> Will Smith, Brother of Hampton Smith,
> Jim Dickson, Farmer, Quitman, G.A.
> and two other Brothers of Hampton Smith.
>
> These names were given to me in confidence by a man who admitted that he was a member of the mob, on the condition that I would not divulge his name, as to do so would cause him a great deal of embarrassment, and probably death.

eon,   subject to the terms
          re hereby agreed to

Hon. Hugh M. Dorsey, Governor,   August 21, 1918   191

Street and No.

Place   Atlanta, Ga.

WILL YOU INFORM US OF ACTION TAKEN, IF ANY, ON MEMORANDUM SUBMITTED
TO YOU JULY TENTH ON BROOKS AND LOWNDES COUNTIES LYNCHINGS. ALL
PATRIOTIC AMERICA AWAITS WITH INTEREST YOUR ACTION IN SEEING THAT
PERPETRATORS OF THESE MOST BARBARIC LYNCHINGS ARE BROUGHT TO JUSTICE.
WHAT CAN WE TELL AMERICA CONCERNING GEORGIA'S GOVERNOR'S COOPERATION
WITH OUR PRESIDENT IN HELPING TO STAMP OUT MOB VIOLENCE?

John R. Shillady, Secretary

NATIONAL ASSOCIATION FOR ADVANCEMENT

COLORED PEOPLE, Seventy Fifth Avenue, New
York

SENDER'S ADDRESS
FOR ANSWER

SENDER'S TELE-
PHONE NUMBER

State of Georgia
Executive Department
Atlanta

August twenty seventh
1918.

Mr. John R. Shillady,

Secretary, New York City, N. Y.

Dear sir;

Referring to your telegrams of
August 21st, and 22nd, with reference to (pic 26th)
the recent lynchings in Brooks and Lowdnes
Counties:

So far as I am able to ascertain no de-
finite results have been obtained in the
effort to apprehend the guilty parties.

I shall take pleasure in advising you
in the event any developments take place.

Yours very truly,

jcg.

Hugh M Dorsey

If you drive to The Little River
near Hahira, Georgia on State Road
122, you will find a memorial
for those who were killed in 1918.
It was erected so the story would
never be forgotten.

We still wait for the arc of the
Moral universe to bend toward
justice. There has never been
a full reckoning of the racial
violence in our country.

Afterword: Hidden Memories

by Julie Buckner Armstrong

Rachel Marie-Crane Williams's haunting graphic narrative *Elegy for Mary Turner* joins a long line of works giving voice to a story that refuses silence.

Mary Turner died on May 19, 1918, during a weeklong spree of mob violence following a white farmer's murder near Valdosta, Georgia. At least eleven African Americans were lynched, including Turner's husband Hayes. Reportedly pregnant and nearing her due date, Mary swore to seek justice against the well-connected mob ringleaders. Her act of speaking out prompted vicious retaliation. Hundreds of people gathered at Folsom's Bridge on the Little River to watch the mob hasng, shoot, and burn the woman—then, according to witnesses, cut the fetus from her body and crush it into the ground.

"Her talk enraged them," a local newspaper explained.

The cruel irony: Turner's murder occurred on Pentecost, according to a Farmer's Almanac page that Williams includes among the narrative's found objects. In Christian traditions, Pentecost marks the day that the Holy Spirit descended on the Apostles in tongues of fire, giving them the power to speak God's message of love in all languages. Turner's lynching, which took place during church hours before several hundred witnesses, spoke loudly about the power of hate.

It also made international news, galvanizing anti-lynching activists and artists of the late 1910s and 1920s, and prompting the National Association for the Advancement of Colored People (NAACP) to investigate. Walter White's resulting exposé, "The Work of a Mob," published in the September 1918 *Crisis*, functions as a key resource for Williams, as it did for sculptor Meta Warrick Fuller and writers Carrie Williams Clifford, Angelina Weld Grimké, Anne Spencer, and Jean Toomer.

These figures formed part of a larger early twentieth-century effort to change public opinion about lynching, seen then as an acceptable form of extra-legal or "frontier" justice. As the NAACP's James Weldon Johnson explained during a speech at the 1919 National Conference on Lynching, most white Americans did not condone lynching, but they did not condemn it either. Yet lynching had less to do with justice than with using violence to enforce white supremacy. The Tuskegee Institute (now University) documented approximately 4,750 lynchings between 1882 and 1968; nearly three-quarters of those killed were African American. Mobs justified their actions by saying they needed to protect white women from Black male rapists. However, less than 30 percent of documented lynchings involved sexual assault accusations, and most of those were spurious at best. More common were incidents where Black people paid the ultimate price for overstepping strict Jim Crow racial codes. Black political, economic, and social success in the decades after slavery's end met with an increasingly virulent white backlash. Large-scale spectacle lynchings, where mob members tortured and mutilated their victims, grew in popularity. These events, which drew men, women, children, photographers, and souvenir hunters, were designed to send a forceful message about who held power's reins, and who did not. Such was the case in May 1918: a lynching rampage that spread out over two counties had its roots in a labor dispute and led to the death of a woman whose only "crime" was speaking her mind.

Mary Turner's story stood out for its barbarism, for the way it revealed lynching's origins in white supremacy, and for the way it embodied lynching's complicated gender dynamics. The rape myth's triangle between white mobs, white females, and Black men had no place for Black women. But they played multiple roles in a larger historical narrative: as victims themselves, as loved ones left behind, and as activists. Their resistance ranged from individual acts of fighting back against daily indignities to collective group action. One organization, the Anti-Lynching Crusaders, used Turner's story as a centerpiece of its fundraising campaign to support the 1922 Dyer Anti-Lynching Bill (which passed the House but stalled in the Senate). Groups such as the Crusaders argued that while female mob victims might be statistical anomalies—roughly .02 percent of all lynchings—their stories still counted.

Williams dedicates her book to those women and children whose deaths by mob violence are largely forgotten.

For decades, Turner was one of those women. Her story became part of what artist Freida High Wasikhongo Tesfagiorgis called in a 1985 painting on the subject *Hidden Memories*. No one actively suppressed this history. Instead, it occupied a liminal space, both present and absent: discussed in pages of out-of-print books or held close by people who did not talk about it publicly. Recovery efforts of the Black Arts and Feminist movements—which focused on the stories and voices of those overlooked in traditional historical narratives—helped to bring "hidden memories" like Turner's to light. In some works, such as the notebook sketches of artist Kara Walker and Alice Walker's novel *The Third Life of Grange Copeland*, Turner's memory remains a faint trace. For writers such as ist Lekethia Dalcoe, Turner embodies a potent force of resistance to Jim Crow violence: Black love.

Like other contemporary artists, Rachel Marie-Crane Williams makes visible what white supremacy tries to erase. The book demands that readers see, that we remember. Williams transports us into memory space in multiple ways. Images evoke the woodcuts and linocuts popular during the heyday of 1930s anti-lynching activism. She sets those images on a background of the past's sepia tones and captions them in an old-fashioned spiky, spiraling cursive—as if we have stumbled onto a scrapbook or memento-filled journal. To create the text's assemblage aesthetic, Williams includes photographs, news clippings, postcards, and letters to remind readers that this seemingly incomprehensible incident occurred in an actual place and time. Especially pointed are drawings of white people going about the daily activities of farm life while mayhem continues around them. "Many were upset, some were ashamed," Williams describes these local white residents, who easily could be the Americans about which

james weldon johnson spoke. neither condoning nor condemning. "But they had pies to bake; they had hogs to feed. Their lives moved forward," the text explains, underscoring how Turner's and other victims' lives did not. Williams further highlights the juxtaposition between the mundane and the extraordinary, the natural and the unnatural, life and death with her use of color and texture. Especially during the lynching scenes, she brings in color washes of black dirt, brown leaves, blue river, and red blood. The site of memory that Williams creates is visceral, raw.

Readers will carry around the stunning images of Williams's *Elegy for Mary Turner* long after turning the book's last page. Turner's story, awful though it may be, deserves that place of remembrance in our hearts and minds. Turner died a brutal death, but she risked her life for justice. A group of men feared this powerless woman's act of speaking out so much that they stole her dignity and her life. Every work of art created in Mary Turner's name repudiates their actions by restoring her humanity to the world.

Postscript:
A Place to Lay Their Heads

by C. Tyrone Forehand (great-grandnephew of Hayes and Mary Turner)

Hayes Turner entered the world in August 1893 in Brooks County, Georgia. He was one of ten children born to John Wheeler Turner, Sr. and Charlotte Gay. In 1918, Hayes was falsely accused of complicity in the murder of Hampton Smith, a Brooks County farmer notorious for his brutal treatment of his farm laborers. Upon hearing that he had been implicated in the death of Smith, Hayes Turner fled. It was reported he had been hidden in a foxhole by his mother, who would sneak food and clothing to him in the dead of night. Following his lynching, Hayes was castrated by those responsible for this heinous act of violence. His father and mother pleaded for the return of his body, but their pleas went unanswered.

His siblings, Joseph, Mary, John Wheeler Jr., George, Julia, Willie, Naomi, and Norman were tormented for many years by the memory of their brother's horrific murder. Questions posed by their children and grandchildren regarding the murder of their brother would always result in an overwhelming sense of sadness, accompanied by a distant and terrifying stare, which led one to believe that they were actually witnessing this dreadful act of terror. A deafening silence would follow as tears began to flow.

Hayes wed Mary Hattie Graham, born in 1885 to Perry W. and Betty Graham. Mary was the second of five children born to her parents. The lives of her sisters and brothers, Pearlie, Perry G., Otha, and Etha were forever changed by the lynching. After speaking out against her husband's murder, Mary took her two small children, Ocie Lee and Leaster, to members of her family for safekeeping. They were reared under assumed names.

Rufus Morrison was only ten years old when he was hiding in a cornfield along Ryalls Road in the town of Barney and witnessed Mary Turner's execution. The memory of a frightened and bewildered woman was forever etched in his mind as he saw the mob tie a rope to her ankles and hoist her upside down from a tree. They taunted and jeered a terrified Mary as they began to roast her alive. One of the shine from a jug and spat it on her as another dared him to slit open her abdomen where her unborn child was oblivious to the fate which was about to befall it. Upon rupturing her womb, the birthing matter which provided nourishment to her unsuspecting baby spewed over three of Mary's executioners. It was reported throughout the years that each of those whom the birthing matter touched died horrific deaths: one shouted on his deathbed, "Get that nigga baby off of me!" After crushing the head of Mary's baby with his boot, one mob member placed his cigar in the jug of moonshine and used it to mark the ground where the life of Mary and her baby were taken. Those who witnessed this violent act of cowardice stated that the sky became dark as the mob completed its task.

There was no place of safety for Hayes, Mary, their unborn baby, or any of the other fifteen victims of the mob mentality that caused the otherwise respectable, law-abiding, Christian men and women of these Southern communities to deteriorate into a pack of roving wild animals bent on destroying the lives of anyone whose skin did not look like their own. Following their violent and brutal deaths at the hands of those who had no shame and never faced justice on this side of life, these powerless and innocent victims of unspeakable human atrocities had no grave to lay their heads.

Today, Hampton Smith, the brutal farmer whose death was the spark that lit the keg of violence in this seemingly peaceful Southern town, has an edifice which stands more than six feet to mark his place of rest in the Pauline Cemetery off of Georgia Highway 133. Descendants of those who executed Mary enjoy roads named in their ancestors' honor, and William Folsom, who owned the property where the lives of Mary and her unborn child were so viciously taken, has a bridge that bears his name as tribute to his contributions to the town of Barney. But one is left to ask, *Who cried for and honored the life of Mary, Hayes, and their baby?*

For many a year, our ancestors have cried out to our spirits, pleading for their stories to be told; today we answer. On Saturday, May 16, 2009, at the Hahira Community Center, nearly ninety-one years following these unspeakable acts of terror, more than 200 people, both Black and white, joined descendants of Hayes and Mary Turner to commemorate this dark stain in our nation's history. The ceremony was organized by those spearheading the Mary Turner Project, a group of faculty and students of Valdosta State University's Women and Gender Studies Department as well as residents of the South Georgia community.

In an interesting twist of fate, or perhaps it was just a coincidence, on the very day of this historic and long overdue event the sky again became dark, as it was reported to have been some ninety-one years ago on that tragic day. More than 100 vehicles caravanned to the location designated by the Department of Transportation as the site for the installation of the marker approved by the Georgia Historic Society. Every oncoming vehicle stopped along the way for the approaching caravan as it moved towards the site of the historic ceremony commemorating the lives of Hayes and Mary Turner and the other victims of the mob violence perpetrated throughout Lowndes and Brooks counties. They commanded the respect in death that they never received in life as the caravan inched ever closer to *a place to lay their heads*.

Here is the text on the historical marker for Mary Turner erected at 4023 GA-122, Hahira, GA 31632:

Mary Turner and the Lynching Rampage of 1918

Near this location on May 20, 1918, Mary Turner, 8 months pregnant at the time, was lynched. Mary was kidnapped and brought to this place for objecting to the lynching of her husband Hayes on May 19. After being brutally killed Mary's body was buried near here in a makeshift grave marked only by a whiskey bottle with a cigar inserted in the bottleneck. Mary and Hayes' murders were part of a larger lynching rampage that unfolded that week in May of 1918. Other victims include Will Head, Will Thompson, Julius Jones, Eugene Rice, Chime Riley, and Simon Schuman, along with two other unidentified victims. No one was ever formally charged in any of these crimes.

(Erected by the Mary Turner Project, Lowndes/Valdosta Southern Christian Leadership Conference, and Valdosta State University's Women and Gender Studies Program.)*

* On October 8, 2020, the Mary Turner Project and the Georgia Historical Society had to remove and store the marker due to repeated vandalism. In its place a large steel cross was erected to temporarily mark the site of Mary Turner's murder.